OLD WATCHET, WILLITON
and around

Watchet — Doniford — Williton — Old Cleeve
and neighbouring places

A pictorial record of the last hundred years,
with commentary by

A. L. Wedlake

The Exmoor Press

First published 1984

ISBN 0 900131 48 9

MICROSTUDIES

Each Microstudy has been written by an expert and is designed to appeal to all who are interested in Exmoor.

The Editor of the Series is Victor Bonham-Carter

A list of all the titles is available from
The Exmoor Press   Dulverton   Somerset

Printed in Great Britain by Williton Printers Ltd., Williton, Somerset.

The Author

Leslie Wedlake was born in Watchet in 1900 and was educated at the denominational school belonging to the Methodist Chapel. Leaving school at the age of 14, he went first as a junior to the Wansbrough Paper Company, then in 1916 to the newly launched Exmoor Paper and Bag Company. In 1919 he went to London and worked for a year in a marine insurance office in Threadneedle Street; but used his spare time to advantage visiting museums and bookshops in Charing Cross Road. He returned in August 1920 as clerk of works to the Cardiff Shipbreaking Company engaged in breaking up the cruiser, *H.M.S. Fox.* Two years later he rented 2½ acres of land from the Wyndham Estate on the Doniford Road, where he started a nursery garden and floral business. Keenly interested in archaeology and local history since a youth, he was elected President of the Somerset Archaeological and Natural History Society 1981-2. He was one of the founders of the Watchet Market House Museum, where a fine selection of his prehistoric finds and old photographs of the locality can be seen. His book, *A History of Watchet,* was first published in 1955 and re-issued with additions by the Exmoor Press in 1973.

Acknowledgements

I wish to thank all those friends who, over the years, have provided me with information, and who have passed on to me so many valuable photographs of historic interest of Watchet, Williton, and the surrounding district: in particular, in this instance, Mrs. Bishop, David Bromwich (of the Local History Library, Taunton), Maurice Chidgey, Dr. Glyn Court, Dr. R. W. Dunning, David Gliddon, H. H. Hole (who has himself written a valuable account in manuscript of Williton), the late Jack Hurley, R. J. Sellick, Mrs. Trebble, and my editor, Victor Bonham-Carter. Some of the posters and notices come from the Stoate family album, kindly lent me by David Gliddon. I am also obliged to Peter Birch (of the Somerset Education Museum), R. Priddy, and Norman Stanley for making a number of photographic prints of original material.—A.L.W.

The photograph on the front cover, taken by Bert Hole, is of the George V Coronation Procession in 1911, emerging from Swain Street, Watchet.

3

Contents

Illustrations

Each source is indicated on the page.
LHL stands for the Local History Library, Taunton.
SEM stands for the Somerset Education Museum.

Kentsford Farm

LHL

Watchet: Origins and Early History

Various relics of early man in the area have come to light—mostly implements. The peoples of the Stone Age in all its phases from c.12,000 to c.2,000 BC used axes to cut timber, arrows to shoot game, and scrapers to flay the hides from animals they killed. Examples of stone tools have been found at Doniford, Cleeve Hill and elsewhere. Towards the end of the Age, man turned from hunting and food-gathering to a primitive form of settled agriculture, taming animals and growing grain. This development was greatly stimulated by the production first of bronze, then of iron, for tools and weapons: which brings us to the arrival of Celtic tribes coming over from the Continent from c.500 BC onwards.

The name of Watchet is thought to have come from the Celtic words *vo-ceto*, meaning 'the town under the wood': which corresponds to the fact that all the high ground would have been wooded around the present harbour site, the latter scoured out by the action of the river and the sea tides between cliffs of hard rock to east and west. A natural harbour was ideal for settlement. Here landed traders and missionaries from Ireland and Wales, some of whom gave their names to local churches: in the case of Watchet, St. Decuman.

The most important event in Watchet's early recorded history was when King Alfred included it among thirty of the most important towns of Wessex. His plan was to thwart Viking raiders by constructing a ring of fortified towns—of which Watchet was one—around his territory: from London along the south coast; then to Exeter, Barnstaple and Watchet (the only place on the Bristol Channel proper); returning inland along the Thames Valley. A number of these towns housed mints, with moneyers striking coins under the authority of the central government. At Daws Castle, the likely site of the Watchet mint, surviving coins indicate AD 980 as the earliest date, and that the mint operated throughout the reigns of nine kings, ending with that of King Stephen—a run of about two centuries.

It was a stormy period. According to the *Anglo-Saxon Chronicle*, the Vikings attacked Watchet three times: in 918 when they were beaten off; in 988 when they laid the place waste; and again in 997. How Watchet fared at the Norman Conquest is not known; it was probably too remote to be directly affected, until its Saxon overlord

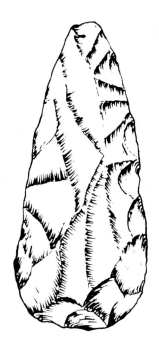

Neolithic Implements

was displaced by a Norman. Watchet is mentioned in Domesday (1086) as belonging to William de Mohun, who built the castle at Dunster. Not long after we find that the local government of the town had become the responsibility of a Borough Court or Court Leet, and that in 1302 it sent two representatives to Parliament. Meeting twice a year it appointed officers such as the Port Reeve, two Constables, a Bread-weigher, and an Aletaster; and exercised considerable powers over fishing, weights and measures, the state of the roads and bridges, petty crime, and public cleansing. Making dung heaps, winnowing corn, sifting ashes, and emptying chamber pots in the streets were a constant nuisance and incurred heavy fines. The Court Leet still has a token existence and meets annually in October.

Like most places in the locality, Watchet was self-supporting in food—fish, meat, grain, and ale, the main beverage. Cultivation was carried out in open unfenced fields, divided into strips—the fields being re-allocated every year so that the good and poor ground should go to each in turn. The 1841 Tithe Map revealed the general pattern; and that, from the Doniford road to the cliff edge, the whole area was one large strip-field known as Culvercliffe. As recently as the 1920s I can remember a number of these strips at Wristland, separated from each other by baulks or banks of land. Arable apart, there were also areas of common pasture reserved for grazing and haymaking, notably at Cleeve Hill and in the valley meadows that run up to Kentsford.

During the Middle Ages important changes of property took place. One of the principal families was the Sydenhams, based at Orchard, Williton. During the 16th century Sir John Sydenham bought the manor of Kentsford, and by his will (dated 1557) bequeathed to his younger son, John, various lands that included the borough of Watchet. After John's death the male line of the Sydenhams at Orchard became extinct; but with the marriage of John's sister and co-heiress, Elizabeth, to Sir John Wyndham, most of these properties were brought together, making a complete manorial entity; and the estate of Orchard received the designation Orchard Wyndham, the name it bears today. Further facts about the Wyndhams are related later in this book.

The parish church of St. Decuman is of ancient origin. It stands high on the ridge that runs from the Doniford valley to Kentsford farm. Its battlemented tower, 80 feet high, overlooks the town and

Coins of the Watchet Mint

the sea, and must have served over the years as an important landmark. The building is mainly Perpendicular Gothic. The interior contains screens, is rich in monuments and brasses, with a chapel, a tomb, and other memorials to the Wyndham family. It is generally accepted that Coleridge had St. Decuman's in mind when he wrote in *The Ancient Mariner:*

> The ship was cheered, the harbour cleared,
> Merrily did we drop
> Below the kirk, below the hill,
> Below the lighthouse top.

A chantry, the Holy Cross Chapel, stood near the harbour until suppressed in 1547. The present chapel of this name is on the upper floor of the Market House Museum building in Market Street.

National events touched Watchet now and then. Visitations of the plague took their toll at fairly regular intervals. With the threat of the Spanish Armada in the 1580s, a local militia was formed to protect each district. Watchet mustered 6 pikemen, 22 billmen and 19 archers, total 52—a large force when compared with that of Weston (super-Mare) which amounted to 7!

There was a remarkable incident during the Civil War of 1642-8. The Royalists held Watchet and on one occasion reinforcements were sent over from Wales, no doubt to help raise the siege of Dunster Castle, also in Royalist hands. However, as the ship approached, the tide was on the ebb, and the vessel was unable to make the harbour. Whereupon a certain Captain Popham, in command of a troop of Roundhead horse, appeared. Popham promptly rode into the shallow water and so plied the ship's party with musket shot that the latter was forced to surrender. The account of the incident ends with 'the greatest rarity of all is that a ship in the sea was taken by a troop of horse'.

KEY TO COINS

Each pair of coins, obverse and reverse sides, as shown opposite, refer to the following monarchs:

First column, top to bottom: 1-2 AETHELRED II, 3 CANUTE, 4 EDWARD THE CONFESSOR, 5 WILLIAM I, 6 WILLIAM II.

Second column, top to bottom: 1-2 AETHELRED II, 3 HAROLD I, 4 EDWARD THE CONFESSOR, 5 WILLIAM I, 6 STEPHEN.

The wooden West Pier with tidal lights as re-built by 1862, but destroyed in the storm of 28-29 December 1900. The iron ore jetty in the centre was built on to the end of the old cob pier which linked it to the town. Contemporary crinolines in the foreground on the East Pier.

James Date

A similar view c.1890. Note the slipway at Splash Point in the foreground.

James Date

Watchet: Harbour and Shipping

From earliest days the men of Watchet would have built some sort of shelter for their ships. These were probably primitive breakwaters, known as 'weres', composed mostly of large boulders heaped together against the prevailing gales. Later the boulders were reinforced with stout timbers driven into the ground, forming a construction called a 'cobb'. The first record of the harbour was in 1458, when mentioned in Bishop Bekynton's Register under an appeal for funds, 'inasmuch as the port is well nigh demolished and utterly destroyed by storms'. Similar appeals were renewed through succeeding centuries, and collections for repairs to Watchet harbour were made as far afield as St. Margaret's, Westminster, and in churches in Yorkshire, Shropshire and Gloucestershire. That there was some sort of pier or jetty in the reign of Henry VIII can be gleaned from a quaint plan of Bristol Channel defences, which shows 'Watchatte' as having a 'were' sheltering three vessels; and in 1564 a Royal Commission spoke of 'Watchet: where small botes have and do use to come yn with Salte, Wyne, etc'.

Towards the end of the 17th century smuggling assumed serious proportions—at Watchet with the entire approval, it seems, of the Wyndham family. William Culliford, Surveyor-General of Customs to Charles II, paid a visit of enquiry in 1662 and reported that Watchet had grown rich on this 'free trade'. The local collector of customs, William Dashwood, was in league with the smugglers, and on one occasion 30 men were at work for two or three hours unloading wine, brandy and cloth (all dutiable), while Dashwood was drinking sack with the master of the Ship Tavern. But by now the port boasted no less than 15 ships trading legitimately and regularly along coast, and across to Wales, Ireland and the Continent. There is a reference in 1673 to a variety of ships and cargoes, including the arrival of 14 chalders of coal in the *Mayflower* from London (a chalder = 1¼ tons). Other goods imported were groceries of all kinds, hides, leather, wine and tobacco; exports included farm produce, paper and timber. One Watchet ship is known to have crossed the Atlantic to Virginia.

Early in the 1700s Sir William Wyndham, lord-of-the-manor and owner of the port, secured legislation to improve the harbour, but the result was described a few years later by Daniel Defoe as inadequate. Meanwhile petitions were going forward for a bye-law

11

The Esplanade in the late 1860s. No railings, but a gas lamp installed in 1867. The invalid in the bath chair was a reputed forebear of the author. Market Street in the background.

James Date

The harbour in the 1860s. East Pier in the foreground. Esplanade House in the centre background. Note the horse and wagon unloading on the harbour floor—before mud made such a job impossible.

James Date

to permit the levying of a duty upon goods passing through the harbour in order to raise reserves of money for future repairs. This was evidence of the growth of trade. Indeed the Watchet fleet so grew that at one time in the 18th century 128 ships were operating from the port—schooners, ketches, smacks, trawlers and brigantines—practically all owned by Watchet people, with familiar names such as John Hurley, owner of the *Good Intent,* Richard Luckes, of *Brothers,* and William Hole of *Social Friends.* There is evidence of recession about the turn of the century—the harbour was silting up, the wooden piles of the east pier were rotting away, and trade was reduced to fishing and the export of kelp; but the bad times did not last.

Halfway through the 19th century trade was transformed by the formation of the Brendon Hills Iron Ore Company in 1853 and the promotion of the West Somerset Mineral Railway to transport the ore to Watchet harbour for transhipment to South Wales—as described in the next chapter. Something however had to be done about the harbour which was in no state to cope with the new demand. After litigation and a public enquiry, the Watchet Harbour Act of 1857 appointed commissioners to take charge. By 1862 a new east pier had been built, and the west pier rebuilt (with a breakwater extension) upon which the mineral lines were laid, and a jetty constructed where ore was tipped direct from WSMR trucks into vessels of up to 300 tons. At the height of the boom in the 1870s, an annual average of 40,000 tons was exported to South Wales in this fashion.

Although the Brendon Hills mines closed down in 1883 under competition from cheaper Spanish ore, and the WSMR ceased running in 1898, trade generally was on the increase. The railway from Taunton had arrived in 1862; holiday traffic, passenger services in steamboats along the coast, and marine excursions multiplied; and general commerce was growing alongside the development of Watchet's own industries. In the early 1890s some 550 vessels a year were entering and clearing the harbour. Then disaster struck. On the night of 28-29 December 1900 a tremendous gale destroyed portions of the harbour and sank about a third of the Watchet fleet. At first the damage seemed too great for the resources of the harbour commissioners. However, undaunted, Watchet people obtained powers to form an Urban District Council (as from 1st April 1902) and proceeded to rebuild, raising capital on the

B & ER saddletank engine on East Pier at some date before 1874. Note early type of disc and crossbar signal. Town slip on left. Iron ore jetty, right background.

James Date

West Pier before 1900. Iron ore jetty extreme right. The two boys are sitting on the 'gridiron' on to which ships settled at high tide so that, between tides, they could be caulked and repaired.

H. H. Hole

security of port revenues and the rates; and despite further damage from another severe storm in September 1903, the work went on. But it was not until the 1950s that the final repayment was made, and that the town was able to say that it owned its harbour.

Most of Watchet's trade between the wars consisted of the import of coal, and of wood pulp and esparto grass for the local paper mill and other mills in the area; and this was revived in 1945. However, the replacement of coal by oil and other forms of energy, and the decline of railway freight, affected harbour trade; and it was not until the mid-1960s that a fresh revival began to take shape. In 1966 the West Somerset Shipping Company leased the West Pier, and then other firms began to take an interest in the possibilities of the port. Now the East Pier has been developed by removing the railway tracks, and by building warehouses and a compound for the container trade. Prominent imports include timber from Scandinavia and Russia, and wine and fruit from Portugal and the Mediterranean. Exports vary, but have run to car parts, tractors and a mixture of smaller industrial goods.

On top of the Town slip c. 1880. Individuals not identified.

15

H. H. Hole

Bert Hole

S99 20 December 1000

Launching of the lifeboat c.1900. Will Lee, *Free Press* reporter, stands in light coat and cap to the left of the ladder. Remains of storm damage in background.

Bert Hole

Watchet Band aboard the lifeboat on the Esplanade on August Bank Holiday 1903. The author is the child in the hat with a rosette at the head of the ladder, his father stands with a clarinet above.

Bert Hole

Two ships brought into Watchet for breaking up after the First World War. *Above: H.M.S. Fox*, former flagship of the Pacific Fleet. *Below: S.S. Dova Rio.*

Bert Hole

Watchet: The Railways

The Mineral Line

The first railway to reach Watchet was the West Somerset Mineral Railway when, in 1857, the line—for freight only—was opened to Roadwater as the first stage in serving the iron ore mines on Brendon Hill. The full story has been told by R. J. Sellick in his two books*, but—as mentioned earlier—the Brendon Hills Iron Ore Company had been formed in 1853, with offices at the bottom of Swain Street in Watchet; and, shortly after, the harbour was re-built to enable the ore to be shipped to South Wales. In 1855 the railway company was incorporated by Act of Parliament and authorised to build a 4 ft. 8½ inch gauge line from Watchet Harbour via Roadwater to Comberow, and thence by incline (at a gradient of 1 in 4) up to the mines on top of the hill. Work began in 1856 and for a time Roadwater acted as railhead to which the ore was conveyed by horse and cart. The incline was completed in 1861.

After the closure of the mines in 1883, the railway continued with a service of two mixed trains daily (passenger and freight) until 1898, when all traffic ceased. A brief revival took place in 1907 when the Somerset Mineral Syndicate was formed to work two of the mines and re-open the railway, though not for passengers. The re-opening was celebrated on 4 July with a gala excursion to Comberow, complete with local officials and the town band. Three years later the venture collapsed, and that was virtually the end of the 'old mineral line'. The rails were removed towards the close of the First World War, and the company was wound up in 1925. The WSMR station house has now been converted into flats, and most of the track up to Washford has become a right-of-way. Traces of the rails can still be seen on the West Pier of the harbour.

The West Somerset Railway and the story of the Brendon Hills Iron Mines (David & Charles) and *The Old Mineral Line* (Exmoor Press).

The Branch Line

The line from Taunton to Watchet and from Watchet to Minehead was built by two separate companies at different dates. The first section of 14½ miles from the junction at Norton Fitzwarren, two miles west of Taunton on the Bristol & Exeter Railway, was broad gauge (7 feet) and completed in 1862 by the West Somerset Railway Company, which had been incorporated by Act of Parliament in 1857. Although the original plan had included

WSMR station c.1875, looking towards the harbour. The tall building at the far end by the level crossing gates housed the Company's offices.

James Date

The WSMR locomotive *Pontypool* about to leave Watchet with a mixed train for Comberow. The horse pulled trucks between the station and the harbour jetty.

James Date

a link with the WSMR, this idea had to be abandoned; and so the WSR constructed its own track to the harbour at Watchet. Thus each line had its own pier — the WSMR on the west, the WSR on the east, as the photographs clearly show. Intermediate stations between Taunton and Watchet included one at Williton, which was promoted to a crossing station in 1871 with an up platform (extended in 1937), and equipped with a water tower and an extensive goods yard. A pleasant facility was provided by the local firm of J. Jones and Son, florists and nurserymen, who sold fruit to passengers from the platform.

The first move to build the second section of 8¾ miles broad gauge from Watchet to Minehead failed for financial reasons. It was not until 1870 that the Minehead Railway Company secured the necessary Act and backing, and completed construction four years later. Both sections were operated by the Bristol & Exeter Railway Company, which however amalgamated with the Great Western Railway in 1876. The latter took over the Minehead Railway in 1897, but the WSR retained its identity until the national re-grouping of railways in 1922. The entire length of the track was converted from broad to standard gauge on 28-30 October 1882.

The arrival of the railway stimulated both passenger and goods traffic all along the line; but particularly at Watchet where the harbour trade rose steadily from the 1880s until 1937, the peak year, when 59,303 tons of goods were handled. Besides this, the station dealt with 15,468 parcels and issued over 22,000 tickets. One of the principal categories of goods involving the railway was the import of wood pulp from Scandinavia for the local paper mill; also esparto grass from North Africa which was forwarded to the sister mill at Silverton, near Exeter. Eventually all this trade was transferred to road transport and, after an uneventful but useful life, the branch line was closed down in its entirety in January 1971. Within a few months a new West Somerset Railway Company was formed and, after a series of negotiations, leased the track and buildings from Somerset County Council which had purchased all the capital equipment from British Railways. Despite difficulties, a seasonal train service was in operation by 1979 from Minehead to Bishops Lydeard, but it proved impossible to agree terms for the run-in to Taunton.

A full account of the line will be found in *Railways Round Exmoor* by Robin Madge (Exmoor Press) and *The West Somerset Railway* by C. R. Clinker (Exmoor Press).

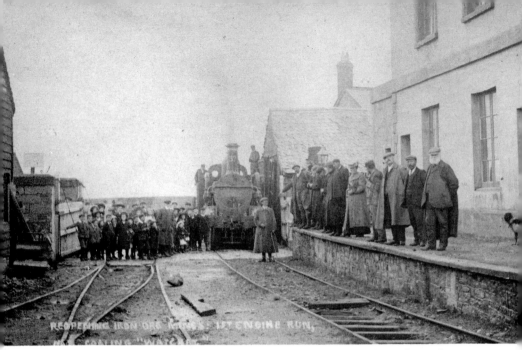

Re-opening of the WSMR in 1907. Coaling the locomotive *Watchet* for the first engine run. From right: Mr. Norris, station master; Henry Kingsbury; Mr. Matthews (with pipe). Standing on the track: Dr. Graham (in long overcoat) talks to W. G. Penny (with arm outstretched).

Bert Hole

Public excursion on 4 July 1907, with local officials and town band on board. Departure was delayed by a storm, but the weather improved in time for a pleasant outing to Comberow.

Bert Hole

Opening of the WSR station in March 1862. Policeman in top hat.

James Date

One of the first trains into Watchet from Taunton, drawn by a B & ER 4-4-0 saddletank engine, No.68.

H. H. Hole

WSR station before 1871, when Watchet was still the terminus of the line from Taunton. In right foreground, at lower level, are the lines leading to the harbour.

James Date

Watchet: Trade and Industry

One of the oldest industries was that of lime burning. The local lias rocks were collected on the foreshore, broken up, loaded into kilns with layers of culm (slack anthracite coal), and then fired. The kilns at Watchet were located at The Cross, formerly called Lime Kiln or Lime Cross. I believe that they were built against the high ground near the present Salvation Army Hall. All traces would have been removed when the WSR station was built in 1861-2, and new kilns set up at Daws Castle, The Warren, and Doniford.

The manufacture of cloth was also of ancient origin, using wool from sheep pastured on the Brendons, the Quantocks, and over Exmoor. There was also a good supply of water for fulling. Types of cloth were often called after the places of manufacture — hence 'Dunsters', 'Tauntons', and 'Watchetts'. Until the first quarter of the last century there was a blanket factory at Doniford, run by John Pulman, one of the Guardians of the Poor Law. Opposite his factory was a field still known as Rack Meadow, and a similar field adjoins the old mill farmhouse in Watchet. In the engraving of Watchet harbour executed by the artist, J. M. Turner, in the 1820s, cloth can be seen spread out in a little field that runs down to the harbour and is called Rack Close.

Milling has been a local industry since Saxon times. Domesday mentions a mill at Watchet, probably the old manor mill at the end of Market Street that operated until the end of the First World War and now a dwelling house. Another small mill at the end of Anchor Street was taken over in 1832 by Thomas Stoate, where he rented both the mill and the adjacent farm and land. Stoate was a man of enterprise. In 1885 he rebuilt and re-equipped the mill, and installed a steam engine and water turbine. The business prospered, but in 1911 the mill was virtually destroyed by a disastrous fire, and the whole undertaking was subsequently removed to Bristol.

Towards the end of the last century a large timber yard and sawmill, operated by John Thorne, extended from the Mill Croft to the railway bridge. Another smaller sawmill on Doniford Road at the top of Goviers Lane was run by John Ennis, who specialised in making shallow boxes for large tin sheets. These were stacked up on the site until there was sufficient for a cargo, and then shipped to South Wales.

Two foundries operated in the town. Gliddons in Swain Street

Stoate's flour mill after modernisation in 1885, when a steam engine and water turbine were installed to augment the previous water wheels, fed by the leat in the foreground.

James Date

Besley's ropewalk in South Road, formerly Mount Pleasant, before the railway station was built in 1862. Wheelhouse in centre.

Bert Hole

had a staff of about a dozen, some of the men coming over from Williton to help out. Much of their work was devoted to making replacements and spare parts for the Paper Mills, the Mineral Line, and the Cliff Railway at Lynmouth; but they also did a lot of iron casting, such as drainage covers, weights for scales, and bearings for agricultural machinery. Chidgeys, the other foundry, in South Road, specialised in making brass bearings, and parts for water wheels and turbines, some of which still exist in farms around.

In the last century a small shipbuilding yard, owned and worked by Benjamin Williams, was located on the edge of Yard Beach— ground now covered by the docks. It was here that Williams built the 140-ton schooner, *The Star of the West*. The last boat to be built was a steam yacht, *Florence,* a 34-foot pleasure boat. In the early 1900s the Jones brothers, shipwrights, could be seen at work— trimming a new mast, or working on one of the ships berthed in the harbour, or caulking a vessel on the 'gridiron' between tides.

An ancient craft important in the days of sailing ships was that of ropemaking, and the Besley family were renowned for their ropes. The early ropewalk was just above the WSR station, but was removed to the Doniford Road when the station was built in 1861-2. In July 1920 the Cardiff Shipbreaking Company opened a yard on and adjoining the West Pier. Here H.M.S. *Fox* was berthed—a ship of over 6,000 tons—and the breaking-up gave much work to a number of men from the town and surrounding countryside over the next two years. Thousands of tons of iron and steel were salvaged, in addition to large quantities of brass, bronze and copper. The company then pulled out, but was succeeded by another shipbreaker, Mr. J. Lee, who brought in a three-masted sailing ship, the *Dova Rio;* but that was the end of the work.

The burning of seaweed was another ancient industry. As early as 1597 there was an agreement between George Luttrell of Dunster Castle and Robert Batten of Watchet, permitting the latter to have all the oare weed between Mouth Bridge and the Warren House for 21 years at an annual rent of 20s 8d. The ashes from the burnt weed were carried by Watchet ships to the makers of glass bottles at Bristol. Alabaster, found in the cliffs west of Watchet, was carved for chimney pieces and church monuments; while gypsum (an inferior kind of alabaster) was also extracted and shipped to South

The staff of John Chidgey & Sons, brass founders and agricultural engineers, who also manufactured water wheels for farms. John Chidgey, wearing bowler and beard, centre left.

James Date

Gliddon's Watchet foundry. Casting 56 lb. weights for scales. Sand for the moulds came from a local river bank.

Gliddon

Wales for the manufacture of plaster of Paris. Some of it was ground fine and used for local paper making.

Paper-making was started at Watchet about the middle of the 17th century by William Wood, who probably made strawboard and coarse paper; but it was not long before he was producing high grade white paper. Several hymn books survive, published by Thomas Hawkes of Watchet, printed on fine watermarked paper. In 1846 the mill was bought by Messrs. Wansbrough, Peach and Date, and it changed hands several times before being placed in the hands of the Receiver after a disastrous fire in 1898. In 1903 the business was purchased by W. H. Reed, though still trading as the Wansbrough Paper Company Ltd. The Reed family had other mills in the south-west. They modernised the Watchet mill, opened a paper bag department and, among other products, turned out a quantity of packing paper and cardboard. The business expanded rapidly and was soon employing several hundred people. The mill now belongs to American interests.

THE PUBLIC

ARE RESPECTFULLY INFORMED THAT

A General Meeting

WILL BE HELD

at the WYNDHAM HOTEL in WILLITON, on SATURDAY the 29th Day of MARCH instant, at 11 o'Clock in the Forenoon, for the purpose of considering the propriety of putting a

Steam Vessel

ON THE COASTING TRADE BETWEEN

Bristol, Watchet, and Minehead;

And if the Measure should be found practicable, a TRADING COMPANY will be formed, and such further steps taken as shall be then determined on for carrying it into immediate effect.

In the mean time, information on the subject will be received or given by

THOMAS HAWKES,

Dated 19th March, 1834.   *Land Agent, &c. Williton.*

Whitehorn, Printer and Bookbinder, Watchet.

29

Wansbrough Paper Mills in the 1860s, overlooked by St. Decuman's parish church.

H. H. Hole

Strong's family fish shop in Anchor Street, c.1880.

James Date

Lime Kiln at Daws Castle, with Harry Gale, the lime burner, and his donkeys.
H. H. Hole

Frank Jones, chimney sweep, outside Sampford Brett church.
H. H. Hole

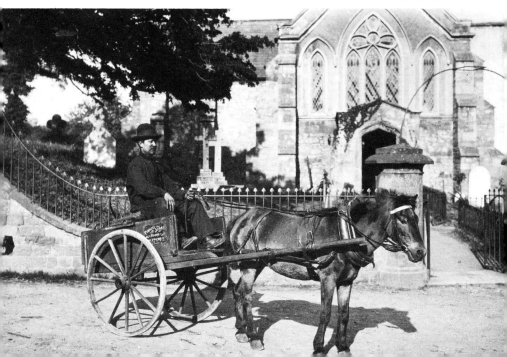

Mail cart at Nether Stowey Post Office. It plied daily between Watchet and Bridgwater.

Capt. H. Brooking

Traction engine and road steamer used to haul pitprops, cut by Portuguese lumbermen in Luxborough woods during the First World War.

Bert Hole

Watchet: Life and People

The Tithe Map of 1841 shows that, at that date, the inhabitants of Watchet were living where their forefathers had always lived — around the harbour. After the 1850s, the boom in harbour trade, the development of industry and general expansion of commerce required the building of many more houses for those engaged in the new sources of employment. The Stoate family appear to have led the way by building The Causway in the 1850s, also six cottages in the Doniford Road called New Buildings. Afterwards came development at Sea View, Almyr, Portland, Gladstone and Wristland Terraces: followed by Malvern Road, Severn and Gilham Terraces. Between the wars new housing appeared at Flowerdale, Temple Terrace, and on the Doniford Road near the old ropewalk. Since 1946 estates have been built at Woodland, Culvercliffe, Kingsland, Reed Close and Greenway; besides bungalows and flats for old people at Maglands and Werren Close. Watchet today covers an area about four times that of a century ago, while the population has risen from less than 2,000 in 1900 to over 3,000.

As to public services — the town was lit by gas in 1867, and a company was formed in 1889 to supply piped water. Electricity arrived in the early 1920s. The Urban District Council, formed in 1902, was recently absorbed by the West Somerset District Council, but Watchet retains a Town Council.

Many improvements to public and social life, especially for the alleviation of poverty and ill health, were due to voluntary effort. For example, in order to avoid dependence on parish relief or transfer to the workhouse, a number of friendly or mutual assistance societies were formed during the 19th century, providing financial aid in sickness and, at death, payment for a decent burial. These societies held annual parades or club walks, attended by colourful ceremonial. Temperance societies also flourished. In March 1890 the jubilee of the Watchet Teetotal Society was commemorated by meetings and a tea. These and older traditional customs tended to disappear shortly before or after the First World War: for instance, St. Decuman's Fair held in August and Watchet Fair in September, both of medieval origin. Caturn's Night on 25 November still survives and is marked by generous consumption of hot cakes and

THE

CORONATION

OF

HER MOST GRACIOUS MAJESTY,

Queen Victoria,

On Thursday, June 28th, 1838.

THIS EVENT WILL BE COMMEMORATED

BY

A Public Tea,

WITH SALT HERRINGS,

To be held on the Green in front of Mr. Royall's House, at Watchet.

As many of the Neighbourhood may wish to attend who are not Subscribers, Tickets, One Shilling each, may be had at Mr. James Dait's, or at Mr. T. Whitehorne's. No admittance without Tickets.

BEEF AND ALE

Will be provided for those who can pay for it.

The Stringston Band will attend.

GOD SAVE THE QUEEN!

WATCHET, JUNE 28th, 1838.

34

cider, accompanied by the ritual repetition of

> Tis Caturn's Night I do believe
> Tomorrow month be Christmas Eve

Other additions to the social life of the town include the creation of the Memorial Ground for sports at Culvercliffe after the First World War, the conversion of the old lifeboat house into a public library in 1953 (the gift of Leonard Stoate), the building of the Red Cross Centre on the Esplanade in 1964, the formation of the Youth Club, et al.

In the old days much of the entertainment and most of the education were provided by organisations connected with church and chapel. Although, by the middle of the 18th century, Watchet is known to have had at least three private schools—one kept by a Mr. Whitehorn in Swain Street, another for young ladies by Mrs. Wheeler at Sea View, and a Dame School above the Market House—it was the advent of Sunday Schools that imparted the greatest impetus. Here young people were taught literacy and strict attention to the precepts of the Bible. Even after the Education Act 1870, denominational schools came into being, e.g. the C. of E. School in South Road, and the Methodist School in the former Station Road. Somerset County Council replaced the earlier Council Primary School with a new building in South Road in 1910.

Mention has already been made of St. Decuman's and the Holy Cross Chapel. The Baptist Chapel was built in 1824 thanks to the efforts of members of Lady Huntingdon's sect. The First Methodist chapel was put up in 1825 and replaced by the present building in Station Road in 1871. The Salvation Army was installed in the old Methodist Chapel as from 1884.

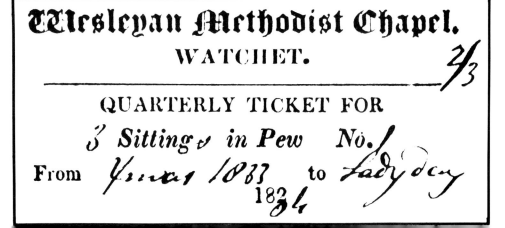

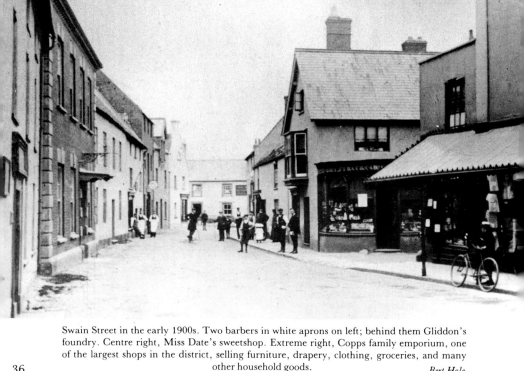

Swain Street in the early 1900s. Two barbers in white aprons on left; behind them Gliddon's foundry. Centre right, Miss Date's sweetshop. Extreme right, Copps family emporium, one of the largest shops in the district, selling furniture, drapery, clothing, groceries, and many other household goods. *Bert Hole*

Market Street at similar date. On left, Thorne's shop selling cycles, boots, shoes, and leather goods. Market House (now the Museum) was Organ's ironmongery. On far right in bowler stands Bill Cornelius, railway ganger, known as 'Billy Go Deeper'. *Bert Hole*

WEST SOMERSET COAST
AUXILIARY
Temperance Society.

This is to certify,

THAT *Mr Thomas Hoole*
is admitted a Member of this Society, having sub-
scribed the following fundamental

DECLARATION:

*WE, whose Names are hereto annexed, do agree,
whilst we continue Members of the Temperance Society, to abstain from drinking distilled spirits, (mixed or unmixed), unless when required as medicine;
to be moderate in the use of all other intoxicating
liquors; to refrain from entering any house for the
sale of such liquors, except on occasions of necessary
business, or when travelling; and to discountenance
the practice and causes of intemperance.*

Thomas Hawker

General Secretary and Treasurer.

N. B. This Ticket admits the Bearer and Friends
to the Meetings of this Auxiliary and its Associations.

☞ *No Person will be allowed to speak irreve-
rently of Religion, or to introduce any topic of a
Political nature, in any Meeting of this Society.*

No. 30,

Whitehorn, Printer.

Some of the young men on
the staff of Copps Stores.

Bert Hole

38

John Griffiths, town crier, parish clerk,
barber, and well-known local character.

Bert Hole

P. & A. Campbell White Funnel paddle steamer at the West Pier, early 1900s.

Bert Hole

Watchet Regatta c.1908. Esplanade House, right centre.

Bert Hole

The Rev. C. H. Heale, Vicar of St. Decuman's, with his baby daughter, Sissie, c.1900.

ALW

Sissie Heale in her donkey cart.

ALW

Interior of St. Decuman's, early 1900s. The organ on right came from Buckingham Palace, having been given by Queen Caroline to her daughter, Princess Amelia, as a birthday present. Later it came into the hands of the Earls of Egremont and was lent to the church by the last Earl, a title of the Wyndham family. When William Wyndham presented the church with a new organ in 1923, this 'royal' organ found its way to Eton College.

ALW

Watchet Rovers football team, 1907-8.

Bert Hole

Wansbrough Paper Mills brass band.

H. H. Hole

St. Decuman's bell ringers, 1910

Bert Hole

Watchet Wesleyan Sunday School.

SCHOLAR'S RULES.

Every Scholar of sufficient age, shall be required to commit to memory the following Rules:—

1. I am to be at the School every Sunday morning and afternoon, exactly at the time appointed.

2. I am to come punctually, with my hands and face clean, and my hair combed.

3. If I enter the School after it is begun, I must take the last place in the class.

4. When at School, I am to be silent, and thankfully attend to the exhortations of the Superintendent, and the instruction of my Teacher.

5. If I neglect School without a sufficient reason, I am to receive such punishment as the Superintendent may think I deserve.

6. If I absent myself without good cause, four Sundays following, or frequently misbehave myself, I shall be dismissed from the School.

7. I am expected to attend the public Worship of God, once on every Sabbath, and oftener if practicable.

8. I am to behave with seriousness, during divine service; and, when kneeling at prayer, keep my body upright, and my hands clasped in a posture of devotion.

9. After the conclusion of the service I am to remain in my seat, until the congregation is gone out; when I am slowly to walk out, and quietly return home.

Balloon flight of Miss Viola Spencer-Kavanagh in 1908. The lady was strapped to a parachute slung below the balloon, and landed at Egrove Farm.

Bert Hole

44

Another view of the 1911 Coronation Procession emerging from Swain Street. Dr. Graham is wearing the top hat. See cover picture.

Bert Hole

M. Louis Salmet, popular French aviator, with his plane at Minehead.

Bert Hole

In 1912 Salmet and his passenger, Mr. Van Tromp, Taunton shirt-maker, crashed into the sea and were rescued by a Watchet crew. They are seen in a car outside Lee's Refreshment Rooms and Thorne's corner bootshop in Market Street.

Vowles

The old limekiln at Doniford.

ALW

Swillbridge House, once the home of 'Stalky'

ALW

Doniford

Only a mile east of Watchet, Doniford has naturally been closely linked with the fortunes of its neighbour. Nonetheless the hamlet fills a small historical niche of its own. Evidence has been found here of prehistoric man, and of a substantial Roman settlement in the fourth century A.D. thanks to the discovery of a variety of pottery, iron nails, and a bronze coin with the inscription of the Emperor Constantine. As mentioned earlier, blankets were made by the Pulman family at Swill Bridge until the early 19th century, and the cloth stretched and dried at Rack Meadow nearby. The ruins of a large lime kiln can also be seen. In modern times Doniford has best been known for the military camp opened after the First World War for Territorials, and enlarged in the 1930s into an Anti-Aircraft Training School, involving the development of a radio-controlled aircraft, called a 'Queen Bee', and used for target practice. Nowadays the camp has become a holiday centre, known as Freshfields.

Another connection, more literary than military, was the residence at Swillbridge House of Major-General L. C. Dunsterville, eminent soldier and the model for Kipling's famous character, 'Stalky', when both were schoolboys at the United Services College, Westward Ho!

'Queen Bee' radio-controlled aircraft.

H. H. Hole

47

St. Peter's, Williton. The cottages once served as the 'chapel house' for brewing ales, sold on feast days to raise funds for church expenses.

H. H. Hole

Old Priest's House, pulled down in 1905 to make way for the present Church Room in Bank Street.

H. H. Hole

Williton

Early man left his mark at Williton as he did at Watchet: visible notably in the Bronze Age barrows at Battlegore opposite Danesfield School, and in the round barrow, known as 'Bloody or Bleary Pate', north of the road to St. Audries. Little else is known about the early history of the area other than that the Saxons occupied West Somerset in the 8th century, and that the Danes raided the nearby coast in the 10th. Incidentally the so-called 'Mother Shipton's Tomb' in Blackdown Wood, that bears the outline of a human face and a Latin inscription is in reality a copy of a Roman sepulchral slab in Cumberland and no more than an early 19th century prank.

The name 'Williton' derives possibly from the brook that runs past the church, or from the larger stream commonly called 'Swilly', which it joins on the way to the sea. Williton is mentioned in Domesday; and farmsteads founded in the 12th century, or even earlier, evolved gradually into a pattern of settlement joined by tracks that—by the Middle Ages—were marked at key places by crosses*: at, for instance, the junction of North, Long and Fore Streets; at the Egremont Corner; and opposite the north porch of the church. Most of the oldest buildings are congregated on the southern and western sides of the town: in Bridge Street, Bank Street (formerly called Priest Street, where stood a Priest's House and an Almshouse) and Half Acre.

The parish church of St. Peter was originally a chapel-of-ease, subordinate to St. Decuman's at Watchet: endowed, it is thought, by the notorious Reginald FitzUrse, one of the four knights who murdered Archbishop Thomas à Becket in Canterbury Cathedral on 29 December 1170. One of his companions was Richard De Brett, a neighbour from Sampford Brett*—thus two aristocratic and historic murderers from the same locality.

But the family that dominated the Williton area was the Wyndhams. Based in East Anglia they rose to power and wealth by a combination of good business, political acumen, and judicious marriages, plus the ability to get back into the saddle when things went wrong: e.g. the beheading of one member of the family for high treason in 1502, and divided loyalties in the Civil War of

*See *The Parish of St. Peter, Williton* by Harry Armstrong, and *The Village and Church of St. George, Sampford Brett* by Dorothy Collins, both privately published.

The Mills and Stream Fields.

MC

Orchard Wyndham, with the Bristol Channel in the distance. An old engraving, revealing a good deal of artist's licence.

LHL

1642-8. It was however the marriage in the 16th century of John Wyndham to Elizabeth Sydenham, owner of the house later known as Orchard Wyndham, that started the saga.

A romantic tale is attached to Kentsford (see photo, p4), where John Wyndham's son, John, lived with his wife, Florence. In 1559 Florence was taken ill, 'died' and was buried in the family vault at St. Decuman's, Watchet. One dark night the sexton tried to steal three valuable rings from the lady's finger; but when blood started to flow from the cut, he ran off in fear, whereupon Florence wakened from her trance and returned home. Moreover her son, born later, was the ancestor of all Wyndhams alive today. The title of Egremont was acquired in 1750 when Sir Charles Wyndham married the daughter of the Duke of Somerset, inheriting the earldom from that source, and made his home at Petworth in Sussex. It was however the widow of the fourth earl who lived at Orchard Wyndham and made many benefactions to the district. On her death in 1876 the property reverted to the head of the Wyndham family; and it was an eventual successor, known as 'William the Seventh', a bachelor who lived at Orchard 1915-50, who is still remembered by older inhabitants. Like the Countess, William made many charitable gifts to Somerset institutions, though few to Williton itself. He was succeeded by his nephew, George, prominent in forestry and local government, who died in 1982. At its peak in the 1840s the Wyndham Estate exceeded 3,000 acres, and in 1980 it still totalled more than 2,000.

Farming was the principal employment hereabouts until recently; likewise the various crafts and industries that served the land and the horse. Wool and cloth-making were also an important source of business at least until the end of the 17th century, and it is known that Williton had a fulling mill, located near where the station road joins the main road. Markets and fairs were long the main centres at which goods and services were bought and sold. The building of inns and the opening of turnpikes were important indicators of the growth of trade. By 1736 there were two inns, by 1787 two more, and in 1800 the Wyndham Arms opened in High Street. Thirty years later came the Wyndham Hotel, replacing a posting house known as the Coach and Horses but later re-named The Egremont. In 1866 The Masons Arms, a former beer house, was rebuilt on the site of the toll house in Shutgate, the old name for North Street. The Foresters Arms has had several changes of name—Railway Hotel

High Street.

Long Street.

H. H. Hole

Bridge Street.

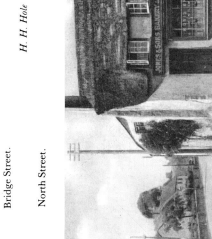

North Street.

H. H. Hole

after the building of the line in 1862 and, before that, The Lamb (1850) and The White Horse (1840).

No less than seven turnpikes were authorised by the Act of 1765, while toll gates surrounded the town at Shutgate, Watery Lane, Wibble Lane, Five Bells, and Tower Hill, surviving at least until 1877 when on 1st November a large bonfire was lit to celebrate their abolition. Five Bells toll house was demolished in 1950 but there is still a Toll Cottage in Long Street. Tolls were good business and were leased for 2-3 years at a time. At an auction in 1872 the reserve price for the Five Bells gates was £302. Charges in the 1830s included One Horse 1½d, One Donkey Cart 4½d, Horses and Waggon 1s 1½d, Horse and Carriage 1s 6d.

By 1851 Williton boasted a bank, a doctor, an architect, two land surveyors, an accountant, and a solicitor. A dozen years later another bank had been added, also an auctioneer, a bus proprietor, a post office, a printer/bookbinder who published a weekly newspaper *(The West Somerset Free Press* had been launched by Samuel Cox in 1860), and a station on the newly-opened railway line between Taunton and Watchet. Other businesses that followed included an organ builder in 1866, an umbrella maker in 1875, a cycle manufacturer in 1897, and an artificial teeth company in 1902—by which time there was a large variety of shops as well. For a note on the photographers, see page 75.

But the principal industrial venture had been introduced in 1833 by John Gliddon when he moved from High Street, Barnstaple, to Bank Street, Williton, which is still the firm's premises today. Starting as a plumber and ironmonger, John Gliddon broadened his activities into blacksmithing and engineering, and by 1859 was selling Hornsby ploughs and washing machines (mangles), and manufacturing his own kitchen ranges. John's sons were sent to good schools and apprenticed to the trade which expanded vigorously; and it was his grandson, Arthur, and the latter's two sons, John and Laity, who helped propel the firm into the 20th century when the motor car replaced the cart and carriage, and the tractor the horse team. The story has continued ever since; and today Gliddons—still very much a family concern—operates a garage and workshop, a hardware store, and agencies for a range of cars, tractors and farm implements, some of which stand on the old auction field across the road. For over 60 years Gliddons ran a foundry, as mentioned earlier, at Watchet for heavy engineering work and castings; but

Bellamy's Corner (now demolished)

H. H. Hole

Half Acre, looking NE

Fore Street, with Post Office in centre

H. H. Hole

Half Acre, looking SW

although this venture closed down after the last war, the firm has since generated fresh business at Barnstaple and at Launceston in Cornwall; but the base remains at Williton.

Another family closely connected with local trade for several generations was the Kerslakes, renowned as blacksmiths, who won many medals and awards for their skill. The story goes that James Kerslake (born in 1834) walked from Halberton (near Tiverton) over the hills to Raleghs Cross, where he tossed a coin to tell him which way to go—Taunton or Williton. Fortune favoured the latter, where James duly set up his forge at Half Acre. All his five sons became blacksmiths, three of them migrated to London, one (Thomas) set up at Washford, while Harry succeeded his father in Williton. Later he took on another forge in Robert Street. His charges were 7d a shoe (which he made), 4d if he used an old shoe, 1d for fastening a loose one. The late Jack Hurley, former editor of the *Free Press,* said that—as a boy—Harry used to trim his hair at the anvil, and made him his first iron hoop with a 'guider' to roll it with. Harry's son Arthur ran a haulage business for 45 years next the forge; and his daughter, Mrs. Maud Trebble, worked for the Post Office as a telephonist—first at Minehead, then at Williton telephone exchange, where she was officer-in-charge for the last twelve years of her service. Mention should also be made of the carriage and wagon works in North Street, that belonged to the Williams family, who were wheelwrights by trade. All traces of the business have long disappeared but a 19th century photograph shows a group of the staff with Philip Williams, the proprietor. One of his sons, Eubulus, became an optician in Taunton; while another, Howard, a man of prodigious memory for local happenings, married into the Kerslake family.

Another local business was that of the jeweller, Tom Bellamy, who succeeded the Thristle family. As early as 1840 James Thristle had established himself as a clock and watchmaker of note; and he made regular rounds setting and winding all the clocks in the big houses. In Half Acre, at the corner of High Street, was Churchills, the saddlers. The small boy in the photo, seen sitting on the fence, is Herbert Henry Hole, who followed his father and grandfather in the family photographic business (see page 75). Albany House in Half Acre was formerly occupied by John Duddridge, hayward and water bailiff to the Wyndham Estate, and in business on his own account as a dealer and haulier. He used mules.

The Forge at Half Acre. Harry Kerslake, centre, James Kerslake (holding child's hand), right, Alex Chidgey, shoeing the horse.

Mrs. Trebble

Harry Kerslake at the Robert Street Forge.

Mrs. Trebble

Although the ancient Court Leet survived until the 1930s, the parish vestry—as elsewhere in the countryside—was long responsible for a number of local services, particularly care of the poor. However, after the Poor Law Amendment Act 1834, a central workhouse serving a 'union' of 35 parishes across Exmoor was built 1838-40 to the design of William Moffat or, as some believe, of the famous Victorian architect, Sir Gilbert Scott. Known as Townsend House, it cost £6,000 to build, accommodated 300 paupers, and survived until the system was abolished in 1948. Nowadays it is partly used as a hospital for old people. In 1894 civil and church administration of local government was finally separated, and Williton became the headquarters of the newly formed Rural District, replaced in 1974 by the larger West Somerset District, thus maintaining the town's role as an administrative centre.

Before the Education Act 1870, such schooling as existed was left to private enterprise and the efforts of religious denominations. Sunday schools were early in the field, most of them starting in the early 19th century. In Williton, Watchet and around, Nonconformists were particularly active—and *strict!* Pupils had to be in class a good three hours every Sunday morning and nearly as long again in the afternoon. Scholar's Rules reproduced here give a vivid impression of the discipline imposed on teacher and pupil alike. Temperance was another cause that aroused strong feelings, although the teetotallers did not have it all their own way. The pioneers of Methodism in Williton were John and Mary Stoate who opened their home for services in 1806 and a chapel in 1820. In 1883-4 a large Methodist church with schoolroom and manse was built on the Taunton road. The late Jack Hurley was organist there.

Entertainment, as at Watchet, was almost wholly home-made, at least until the First World War. Music was provided by the drum and fife band; and plays were produced by Miss Ellen Heathcote, daughter of the vicar, a 'character' who also grew fine violets. In her will she forbade the use of a hearse, and so her coffin was borne to the churchyard in a builder's lorry. A circus used to visit Williton at intervals and put up its tents and cages in a field now occupied by the County Surveyor's Department in Long Street. The photo on page 63 shows Ben Gliddon (a son of John) with a circus elephant, probably in Long Street. Was this the pachyderm that, when his guardian was arguing the price with the toll keeper, calmly lifted the gate off its hinges and walked through uncharged?

North Street Carriage and Wagon Works. Proprietor, Philip Williams (with beard and
bowler) stands next to the circular saw.

58

Right to left: Harry Kerslake, Alex Chidgey, James Kerslake, Anon.

Five Bells Toll House, on road to Watchet, pulled down in 1950.

ALW

Advertisement by Gliddons in the *Free Press* of 25 August 1860.

Gliddon

Flooding on the broad gauge line at Williton Station, November 1877.

H. H. Hole

Soldiers leaving Williton after enlisting in 1914.

H. H. Hole

WILLITON DRUM & FIFE BAND.

Drum and fife band. Rev. C. H. Heale on left. Alfred Wedlake in centre with cap, conductor.

ALW

Yeomanry Camp at Torweston Farm.

H. H. Hole

Townsend House.

H. H. Hole

Garden Fete at Eastfield, 1908.

H. H. Hole

Circus elephant in Long Street. Ben Gliddon on left.

Gliddon

Manual Fire Engine — in action until late 1930s.

Bert Hole

The men who built the Methodist Church at Williton 1883-4.

H. H. Hole

Contrast in styles of transport outside the Egremont Hotel in the 1920s.

H. H. Hole

Old Cleeve and neighbouring places

The parish encompasses nine villages and hamlets, and numerous farmsteads; and it has a crop of historical associations. Old Cleeve itself — the name derives from the high cliffs overlooking the Bristol Channel — is mentioned in Domesday. The parish church of St. Andrew, a fine Gothic building at the east end of the village, was begun before the foundation of Cleeve Abbey in the 'Valley of Flowers', south of Washford, and the arrival of the Cistercian monks in c.1198. The Cistercians were industrious farmers, kept sheep and reclaimed land. Their great abbey — the only one of the Order in Somerset — and its attendant buildings covered some 30 acres, but then steadily disintegrated after the Dissolution in 1537. The abbey church itself has long disappeared, but the buildings that remain are now well cared for, an impressive reminder of an active life under the monks for close on 350 years.

Another building of ecclesiastical origin is at Chapel Cleeve, north of Old Cleeve, where a chapel dedicated to the Blessed Virgin Mary was the object of pilgrimage in the Middle Ages. Originally the chapel had been built on the cliffs but, following a landslip, had been rebuilt inland. The 'miraculous' escape of the statue of St. Mary during the disaster had not only attracted devotees, but prompted Edward IV to grant the Abbot a licence to hold a weekly market and two annual Fairs, thus assuring considerable sources of income. The chapel was served by a hospice or inn, and this was incorporated in a house built by Richard Carver 1818-23, later enlarged, and now converted into an hotel.

Yet another building with religious associations is at Leigh Barton, Leighland, once the home of the Poyntz family, who adhered firmly to the Roman Catholic faith after the Reformation. They sheltered and supported a priest, Don Philip Powel, until his betrayal and execution in 1645. The old chapel still exists in a detached block behind the farmhouse, the latter having been rebuilt in the classical style about the year 1809. See the article by Berta Lawrence in the *Exmoor Review 1984*.

There are several other houses of historical interest in this area, as the following examples show.

One is Bardon House (strictly in the parish of St. Decuman's, Watchet, but it has always 'looked' towards Washford) — the scene of a strange tale related in Jack Hurley's *Legends of Exmoor* (Exmoor

Old Cleeve village and church tower.

VBC

Chapel Cleeve

H. H. Hole

Press). For generations it was occupied by the Leigh family. One day in 1836 it was reported to Robert Leigh that a dove was repeatedly beating against — and breaking — an attic window pane. Leigh went upstairs and found an old box containing State papers that related to the intrigues of Mary, Queen of Scots; and in particular to the plot of Anthony Babington to murder Queen Elizabeth I — events that led up to Mary's execution in 1587. Was the dove Mary's spirit desperately affirming her innocence? The documents were duly acquired by the British Museum in 1870.

At Bilbrook, on the main Minehead road almost opposite the turning to Old Cleeve, stands a substantial and handsome building that has had a remarkably chequered history. Put up in the early 1700s by two brothers named Harris out of profits from smuggling and ship-wrecking, it became an inn, 'The Green Dragon', and then passed into the hands of James Symons, a convert to Methodism and who opened the house for preaching in 1794. James ran the first stage wagon between Minehead and Bristol, sold general merchandise and — supported by his son and grandson, both named William — turned the Green Dragon into a centre of Methodist activity and assembly. Grandson William was an apothecary and the author of *Early Methodism in West Somerset and the Lorna Doone Country* (Kelly).

Then there was the mystery of Croydon Hall, a large house south of Rodhuish and now a special school for maladjusted children of junior age. The mystery attached to a former owner, not to the house. Jack Hurley has told the story in his *Murder and Mystery on Exmoor* (Exmoor Press). Before the First World War the Hall belonged to Count Conrad von Hochberg, a rich and good-natured German aristocrat, a member of the royal house of Pless. He was an undoubted Anglophile, staunch Anglican, hunting man, and benefactor of many local causes. Suddenly, in the middle of the hot summer of 1914, Archduke Ferdinand of Austria was shot at Serajevo and war threatened — although not many people in West Somerset took the threat seriously, not even apparently Count von Hochberg who, as late as 24 July, gave a big garden party at the Hall and seemed as affable and unconcerned as ever. On 4 August however, war was declared between Britain and Germany, by which time the Count had disappeared. All kinds of spy rumours were circulated, despite the denials of the Rector of Old Cleeve, a personal friend to whom von Hochberg had confided that he was

The Refectory at Cleeve Abbey before restoration. Note the crucifix on the far wall—part of a *fresco* that has now disappeared.

H. H. Hole

Leigh Barton chapel—east end.

VBC

volunteering for Red Cross service in Germany. In due course the property and its entirely innocent contents were seized by the Crown, and the rumours retreated. The Count never came back. When he died after the war, he was buried in Berlin, but the funeral service was conducted in English according to the rites of the Church of England: by which time the parishioners of Old Cleeve had been so foolish as to remove the Count's coat-of-arms from a bench end in the church. What did the Count look like? There is a glimpse of him here in what is, perhaps, an unique photograph of his sojourn at Croydon Hall.

At Roadwater the Methodist interest was always strong, thanks notably to the Court family. In the *Exmoor Review 1983* Dr. Glyn Court referred to his grandfather, William, a shoemaker, who became a noted local preacher in the Bible Christian circuit (a revivalist movement that later fused with the mainstream of Methodism). William's elder son, Lewis, became a minister and was the author of *The Romance of a Country Circuit* (Hooks). The younger son, Will, Dr. Court's father, kept the post office-cum-shop in Roadwater, specialising in the repair of boots and cycles. An excellent source of information about this area is Dr. Court's own book, *West Somerset in Times Past* (Countryside Publications). Washford, another Methodist stronghold, is remarkable for its imposing chapel standing beside the main road. Opened in 1826, it was for many years the largest in the Dunster circuit, renowned for its Sunday school and as a centre for revivalist meetings.

High up in the Brendons, but part of the united benefice of Old Cleeve, the hamlet of Treborough seems remote and empty. The church of St. Peter is a stark solitary building, in the Perpendicular style, with a pyramid tower roof. There is a cross in the churchyard. The graves are evidence not only of local farming families, but of men who came from Wales and Cornwall to work in the iron ore mines on Brendon Hill; and of others employed in the large slate quarry gouged out of the ground on the way down to Roadwater and now being filled with County Council rubbish. Opposite is the Nature Trail constructed by the Exmoor Natural History Society.

Old Cleeve has always been predominantly agricultural. In the past the manufacture of cloth was the main employment outside farming: a tradition sustained today by the old established firm of J. Wood & Sons, sheepskin processors, who make fine lambskins and rugs, some of which were made up for a wedding present for Prince

Bardon House.

H. H. Hole

Baby Show at Croydon Hall, August 1908. Count von Hochberg wearing trilby and gaiters, and looking down—probably using a camera.

H. H. Hole

Charles and Princess Diana. Small industries that have vanished include a tannery at Linton, cement making at Warren Farm, and the extraction of alabaster at Blue Anchor. But the principal phenomenon over the last hundred years has been the growth of the holiday industry, stimulated by the introduction of steamer trips in the Bristol Channel, the construction of the railway line between Taunton and Minehead, and development along the coast. Blue Anchor (or Cleeve Bay) was described in the early issue of the *Free Press* as having 'some capital places for bathing . . . the air is salubrious and bracing, and the views extensive and picturesque'. In fact plans for development were put forward as early as 1862, involving the construction of about 150 villas and cottages on either side of the Blue Anchor Hotel, graced by a church and public gardens. Nothing further was heard of this scheme; but the present caravan park would not have been possible without the massive sea defences in the form of 750 yards of sea wall and promenade, first taken in hand by the County Council about 80 years ago. The first wall, completed in 1901, cost nearly £17,000, and by 1925 the bills for repair and maintenance had amounted to a further £61,000, making it 'the most expensive road in the county to maintain'. Nor did necessary work and expenditure stop there, but that is another story.

Treborough slate quarry.

H. H. Hole

Thomas James Kerslake (brother of Harry) who operated the forge at Washford.

Mrs. Trebble

Will Court's shop at Roadwater.

Dr. Glyn Court

Threshing near Washford.

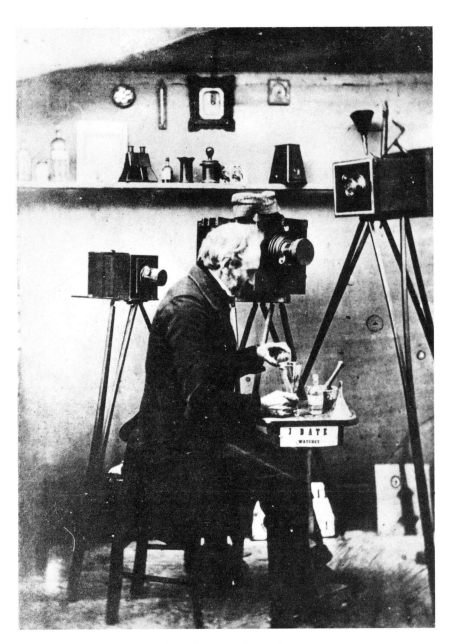

James Date—a self-portrait.

The Photographers

In his book, *The Old Mineral Line,* and in the *Exmoor Review 1977,* R. J. Sellick wrote about some of the early photographers, a number of whose prints are reproduced in this book, and copies of whose work (sometimes the original glass negatives or plates) are in private collections, or are held in the Museum in Watchet or at the Somerset Education Museum at Taunton. The following is an extract of the information provided by Mr. Sellick with additional notes by Mr. Hole, of Williton.

James Date lived at Myrtle House in Swain Street, Watchet, and probably took to photography as an amateur. At some time between 1861 and 1866 he set up in business as a 'photographic artist', which he combined with letting apartments. Few of his negatives survive, but by good fortune he made an album of his work for his grand-daughter who bequeathed it to her niece, Mrs. Dorothy Lyddon, of Minehead, and with her kind permission copies of many of his photographs were made. Date died in 1895, but in 1877 he had sold the business to Herbert Henry Hole, who started in Long Street, Williton, in 1856 as a printer, bookbinder and stationer, having learned his trade in Bridgwater.

Two years later Hole took to photography full-time, built a 'glasshouse' studio behind his shop, and concentrated at first on portraits. Subsequently he took a large number of views and recorded many local events, opening a branch in Minehead as well as maintaining Date's former business in Watchet. After his death in 1900, Minehead was kept going by his elder son, Frank, until the latter's death in 1911. The Williton studio was run first by his widow and then by his younger son, Walter. Ultimately the business passed to Walter's son, named Herbert Henry after his grandfather, until retirement in 1974.

A separate photographic enterprise was operated in Watchet by Bert Hole, son of the original Herbert Henry's first marriage, and who set up on his own at some time between 1894 and 1897 and continued until his death in 1935. Competition between the two firms was keen, but Bert Hole concentrated in the main on topical postcards, and it was he who took most of the subjects connected with Watchet Harbour, the railways, and the revival of the mines after the turn of the century.

Another early photographer, whose work is not however reproduced here, was Daniel Nethercott, a Roadwater man, born in 1829. He first became a stone mason, but later trained as a photographer, and built a darkroom and studio at the family farm at Druid's Combe, where he undertook whatever work was offered, including shots of the mineral line. Nethercott died in 1918.

PHOTOGRAPHIC GALLERY,
LONG STREET, WILLITON.

H. H. HOLE begs to call the attention of the inhabitants of Williton and its neighbourhood, to his superior Ivory-toned Ambrotype Portraits, possessing all the delicacy of Daguerreotype, without the usual Metallic glare so much objected to; they do not fade, and will bear washing like a piece of porcelain.

Family groups artistically arranged.—Drawings, &c, accurately copied.

STEREOSCOPIC VIEWS AND PORTRAITS.
Portraits for Rings, Brooches, Lockets, &c.

H. H. H. returns his sincere thanks for the very liberal support he has received in this branch of his business during the last two years, and hopes by well-developed and life-like Portraits, combined with moderate charges, to merit a continuance of their patronage and recommendation.

N.B. —Lessons given in Photography.

☞ A complete *PHOTOGRAPHIC APPARATUS*, *for sale, (warranted.)*

Advertisement in the *Free Press*, 3 November 1860.

H. H. Hole